HEART

OF

LEADERSHEEP

HEART
OF
LEADERSHEEP

PROTECTOR OF ALL THINGS SMALL
(SHEPHERD'S JOURNEY AND LAMBING 2015)

CHERI MAGNUSON

ARPress
45 Dan Road Suite 15
Canton MA 02021
 Hotline: 1(888) 821-0229
 Fax: 1(508) 545-7580

Ordering Information:
Quantity sales. Special discounts are available on quantity purchases by corporations, associations, and others. For details, contact the publisher at the address above.

Printed in the United States of America.

 ISBN-13:   Softcover   979-8-89389-797-5
                    eBook   979-8-89389-798-2

Library of Congress Control Number: 2024923375

This book is dedicated to

Icelandic Leadersheep, often forgotten and underestimated.

The ISBONA shepherds that have been there for me with advice and encouragement.

My grandson Fletcher and his friend, Josh who were there when I needed them.

My granddaughters Christine, Cheyenne, and their mom Jennifer, who are inspirations to me.

The State Fish Hatchery man that saved Glimmer and Finni from certain death.

The wonderful ladies of the Enfield Town Office who let me use their computer.

Janet who gave me the strength when I was so sick to help Ulle and her lamb.

Cathy the good Shepherd who was always there with encouragement and prayer.

Brittany, the voice of reason during the storm and my strong right arm.

Finally, to the Lord who has been with me, through all the sorrows and joy.

Heart is my big, beautiful, intelligent Leadersheep that lives on Coldstream Icelandic Sheep Farm. It took me three years to figure out why she never lambed. I just thought she was just waiting for her Prince Charming. Four different rams came through the farm and left without a lamb for her. I know that she loved lambs because she was present for each one's birth. After the lambs were born Heart would continually watch over them and protect them. All the lambs love their Auntie Heart and played around her every day, they often showed off in their lamb races. Sometimes Auntie Heart would spring along with them as if her legs were Pogo Sticks. It was hilarious watching a 200-pound ewe bouncing around with the lambs.

I had a veterinarian examine her a few years ago to try and figure out why she never lambed. She told me that Heart could never lamb because her gender was not defined. After that revelation I took her name off the breeding ewe flock and gave her the position she had deserved all along. Heart the Leadersheep: Protector of all things small.

THE AUTHOR

CHERI MAGNUSON

I am a Shepherd of Coldstream Icelandic Sheep in the beautiful State of Maine. Retired from Aerospace Engineering in 2013, I purchased a small farm in Maine to follow a dream that has been with me since I was a young girl. My dream was to have a little farm with a clear, clean, rushing stream running through it. A healthy woodland full of all kinds of beautiful trees. The most important part was the lovely meadows where wildflowers grow and a flock of beautiful, colorful sheep. My dream has become a reality. The journey has been one full of joy and sorrow.

The year my first lambs were born, my son took his own life. I found that writing eased the pain and has given me a new focus. Writing gave me a meaningful existence. So now I share my dream and the journey of life on my farm with others. Other people who may also have a dream yet to be. This is Heart's story. Who knew, when I first saw this tiny lamb with the sweet smile that she would become Heart the Leadersheep: Protector of all things small.

This is the Story of not only Heart and her flock, but my journey as a Shepherd as well. Most of this book is taken from my journal and Facebook posts about life and death on a farm, the sorrows, and the joys. Through it all I express my Faith in God and journey of life living my childhood dream.

INTRODUCTION

In 2013 the company I worked for had been bought out and all of us near retirement had decisions to make. We were offered a package for early retirement. I was sixty-three years old and instead of being fearful, I embraced it with open arms. This package made it possible for me to buy a little farm and some sheep somewhere. I started researching different states, their topography, drought patterns, aquifers, canopy, streams, lakes, and weather. I also researched any hazards or polluters like nuclear plants, mining, if there was any fracking, chemical plants, and industries. A Healthy organic movement was important to me too. The prices and availability of good farmland would be important. I narrowed it down to Vermont or Maine. Vermont was lovely, but Maine had that beautiful coastline and a diverse forest that covered over eighty percent of the area, plus thousands of clean streams, ponds, and lakes. So, Maine it was.

Then I started researching breeds of Sheep. I wanted a triple purpose sheep. That would be sheep that you could milk, eat, and that had a beautiful, soft fleece in a variety of colors. After reading about the Canadian woman who was the first to bring Icelandics into North America, I knew I had found my breed of Sheep. It would have to be Icelandics, the Viking sheep. These sheep came with the Vikings on their exploration and settlement of so many islands and continents. Without the sheep, there would be no Vikings. They made the sails of their ships from wool, as well as their clothing, tents, and blankets. Icelandic sheep are descendants of these sheep. The breed is over a thousand years old and very pure. They are hardy, intelligent, have amazing fleece that is double-coated and comes in so many shades of autumn, black, and grey, plus all the lovely patterns.

My first purchase was a lovely black polled ewe named Everdeen. When I saw all her long, shining black curls and those big expressive eyes, I just had to have her. I also purchased her half-sister, Glimmer, so she could have a (best friend forever (BFF) to grow up with. Each farm I purchased my foundation flock from, I researched the lineage. Everdeen and Glimmer had Tongue River, Jaeger, and Yeomen lineage, which were some of the foundation stock first brought into North America. Everdeen was a direct descendant of the famous Saddleback ewe. Everdeen's mother was a (Moorit) brown and white spotted ewe. Her sire was a champion white-patterned ram that was a rich, golden color with wide horns. I found out later that some people frown on breeding Horned with polled because the lambs born from that cross can have wonky horns or scurs. Maybe I will get her a polled ram to have her lambs with, time will tell.

The Leadersheep bloodlines and history fascinated me. Red Brick Road in Illinois had several lambs with some Leadersheep bloodlines on their website. I looked at the pictures and I fell in love with (Kersha) Heart and (Korah) Ulfa. Heart was a Triplet and ended up being my smallest ewe for a while. Even so, she had a big personality. She was adventuresome and inquisitive, nothing got past her or Korah (Ulfa). Korah was a special color called Single Gene Gray Mouflon or SGGM. All sheep with this coloring trace back to Xeno on Fence Row Farm. I was so excited to have an SGGM in my flock. SGGM was very rare and Xeno was the first one born in North America. Korah's sire was Jupiter, son of Xeno. Her mother was an RBR Glimmer a black and white spotted Leadersheep. Because Korah's mother was spotted, there was a chance that she could have spotted SGGM lambs. They would be so beautiful!

When I was researching Icelandic Sheep Flocks in North America, I had a few favorite flocks and Fence Row in Michigan was one of them. Marti Favre had an ewe named Sienna that I dearly loved. She had done very well in the shows and was such a beautiful auburn color. I was able to purchase her twins, Faith and Hope. Faith was a gorgeous black grey and Hope was white patterned, which looked pure white. Sienna's lambs were very chunky with excellent conformation and fleece. They were perfect ewes for a foundation flock. Their sire was Growler, a son of Keivkur.

Heart and the smile that stole my Heart 2013. Her name was Kersha when I bought her, but she is now called Heart. She was named Heart not just because of the Heart on her nose, but because of that sweet smile and loving eyes. Who could resist this darling little ewe? In the beginning when she and Korah (also known as Ulfa) first came to Coldstream Farm, Heart was tiny. So tiny that some of the other lambs picked on her. Ulfa decided to be her big sister and watch over her. She wouldn't put up with anyone butting her BFF and would quickly put them in their place. As time went on, Heart grew and established her place in the flock as Nanny of all the lambs. She watched over and guarded the ewes as each one lambed. She was the first flock member to check the new lamb out.

THE JOURNEY HOME
WITH OUR FLOCK

November 2013

The Journey to pick up our lambs did not go according to plan. Our truck continually broke down and I was at my wits end. I often turned to prayer and a few times cried. Even so, I felt that Angels watched over us and protected us along the way. Here are some journal entries on the road to get my little flock.

The tire we fixed blew out on the way home from the seller. We took the truck down to Bangor and put new snow tires on it. I think the tires that were on it were defects and I don't want to take chances with my ewes.

We are on the road again. Will be in PA to get the girls early in the morning. We are driving at night and will be taking the toll roads. Keep us in prayer. Then it will be on to MI to pick up Faith and Hope. I will drive during the day.

The truck died again. We are in Falls Creek, Pennsylvania. Things were going so well. Not sure what to do now. I don't know if they tow with sheep on board. We have Everdeen and Glimmer in the back, and I don't want anything to happen to them. Father God, I am weary of these trials. What am I supposed to learn from this? Thank you for being at a rest stop. I do appreciate that. I am not leaving my sheep here alone in the parking lot all night.

The tow truck driver was so careful loading our truck onto the flat bed. He gave us a ride to the motel, which was just across the road from him. When Eric went to check the lambs in the morning, the mechanic's families were there feeding the lambs graham crackers and petting them. They had filled the water bucket too. Our Southern girls are so friendly, Laura Frasier brought them up right. Hehehe.

We had to have the truck fixed again. It died on the Ohio Tollway. All the lights went out, so we had no power. Eric was able to coast it off onto the side. Every time an 18-wheeler roared by in the pitch-black night, our truck would shake. I started to cry. "Mom don't cry, you're a warrior, be strong, and don't let fear take hold of you. Everything is going to be okay!" A tow truck arrived and loaded our truck again. This driver was also very careful of the lambs.

We now have all new fuses and a timer thing. Marty is going to meet us at a rest stop with Faith and Hope. Marty Favre is a sweetheart. She helped load Faith and Hope. They are big and beautiful. We are on our way to Red Brick Road to pick up (Korah) Ulfa and (Kersha) Heart now. Terri has a lovely place. I got to see Ulfa's and Heart's mothers too. On the road again with the lambs. All the lambs are warming up to us. Hope is still a bit shy. Those farm girl's lambs are so social. They are the first in line for treats and the most vocal. Glimmer is sick of the truck though. She butts the canopy now and then. It seems to stress her more than the others being cooped up in a small space with strange sheep.

Hard to believe we are finally home. The girls were out of the truck in no time. Glimmer hopped out first and started eating bushes. All these beautiful pastures and they are eating brush and weeds. Heart and Ulfa are not in the picture, they are already scouting out the pastures. Leadersheep even as lambs, they are so brave and curious. All the girls are sticking with the farm BFF they came with. When I purchased them, I made sure each one would have a friend to grow up with. I wonder if they will always have that bond. Korah, my Leader ewe, has decided that the girls cannot bully little Heart anymore. She is protecting her like she was her own lamb. Yeah, Korah, good girl.

First day on the farm with my little flock. Hard to believe my dream came true. They bonded with each other, Eric, and me on the journey. The FAV twins are nearly twice as big as my other girls. I will not be buying a ram until next year, so they will all have time to grow. I have a lot to learn about Icelandic sheep, lambing, and all kinds of things. We are on a journey together, my little flock and me. There is such a peace here in this place. I look out over the meadows and see there are trees in shades of red and orange in the woodlands. Autumn is my favorite time of year. I feel so very blessed and thankful we have all made it through our journey safely. We are home.

My daughter posted. From Jen Moran:

Ahhh, look at your reality. No more dream. You have it. You fought for it and it is yours. I'm so proud to say you are my mother. You are so strong and amazing! I love you and we miss you!

The affirmation from those we love makes our hearts smile.

November 2, 2013 in Enfield, Maine

First snow this year and it is blowing sideways. The snow is rather fine. I see the wind keeps changing directions. So glad the indoor coop is done but wishing I had moved the chickens last night. I will get Ethan to help me today. All the red hens are laying now. I hope they lay all winter. I put a light in the coop and there is a big window that brings light in too. Farm fresh eggs are so yummy no matter what season.

November 2, 2013 in Enfield, Maine

November 30, 2013

My sick lamb, Glimmer. We have her in the mudroom now. I am warming up the Penicillin so I can give her a shot. I am also mixing molasses with water to give her to drink. Glimmer is so sick. She contracted shipping fever from the stress of the long journey. Eric carried her into the mudroom for me. I put a tarp on the floor with some newspapers and hay on top of it. After consulting with my fellow shepherds, I mixed Red Cell and Pedialyte together and hand-fed it to Glimmer with a bulb syringe. She had shots of antibiotics too. Glimmer *bahed* into the darkness last night and I answered with a *bah* back from my room. I guess she wanted to make sure she wasn't alone. It became our routine the week she spent in the mudroom recovering.

December 2013

Well, Glimmer jumped over the baby gate today and walked into the living room to find me. I guess she is better now. Eric put her back in the barn with her flock mates. Her sister Everdeen was so happy to see her. She was sick a week and it was touch and go. So thankful that she made it.

December 2013

Winter, December 2013

Snowfall, and the ewes are butting heads with gusto. I worry about Everdeen, she has no horns but still stands up on hind legs and crashes down on Korah or Faiths horns. Maybe I should buy her a Viking helmet? Hahaha. There are all feeling frisky in the crisp, cold weather. There will be no ram until next fall, I want them all to be mature. It will give me time to learn the ropes as a Shepherd too. So thankful I have the Icelandic Breeders of North America (ISBONA) to bounce questions off. This is a learning experience, for sure.

Last night I watched the snow, mesmerized by the ferocity of the dance. It was glittering and blowing sideways, suddenly changing direction, and blowing the opposite way. A whirlwind of snow would spin then throw the snow in all directions. I thought we would probably lose power, but we didn't. This morning, the sunlight was shining on the bright clean snow, sparkling like millions of tiny diamonds.

Storms always bring memories from my childhood back to me. They warm my heart and make me smile. I remember the sounds and smell of the sea after a blustery storm, when my grandfather and I would look for treasures brought to us by the waves of the storm. Sometimes there would be glass fisherman's floats in shades of blue and green. We always found driftwood in so many marvelous shapes. Oh, and the shells—so many kinds and colors and shapes. My favorite part was the grey-haired man with twinkling blue eyes and Tam smiling and laughing with me.

DANCING DIAMONDS

Dancing diamonds in the snow today,
As the sunlight streams across the meadows.
Snow is crunching beneath my boots as I walk to feed my sheep.
Dreams are birthed and some dreams die, or so it seems to me.
Is this where I am supposed to be or am I lost in time?
Hours and days have passed me by, so many I have wasted.
But this moment while I watch the dancing diamonds in the snow,
I smile and think, who is to say what time is really wasted?

Eric came in, excited with good news. Korah, my single gene grey ewe has finally let him rub under her jaw and scratch her back. He calls her Wolfie because of her color, I guess. He said she was kicking her back leg like a dog while he scratched her back. I think Ulfa, which means Wolf in Icelandic, would be a better choice for her name. Eric agreed.

Eric separated Ulfa and Heart from the rest of the flock today. Heart is coughing a little today and her stool is a little loose. I am going to keep her in the barn with Ulfa and take her temp. I went into the house to get the B12 Complex and came back to a strange site. Ulfa had jumped over the gate and Heart tried to push out to be with her. She got the gate stuck on her horns. When I went out, she was walking around with the gate on her head. "So, Heart would you like me to take that off your horns?" I guess baby gates are for babies, not Icelandic Sheep. After talking with some shepherds, I gave the girls some Selenium E Paste and Red Cell. I started them on Organic Kelp too. Viking sheep survived harsh winters for hundreds of years eating seaweed. Their system needs it, I guess. So much to learn, I hope they all survive my lack of knowledge.

I can't believe how beautiful my sheep are. Their fleeces have grown out and are so thick, yet plush. I think Faith is the prettiest with her silver fleece and the way she carries herself so regally. Faith, Ulle, and Ulfa all have similar builds and fleece. They hold themselves in a proud manner. Glimmer, the warrior princess, is fierce and gorgeous. She hates chickens though. I have no idea why. I hope they stay on the other side of the fence from her. Everdeen is coal black and has a fantastic fleece. She is super sweet, like a lap lamb. I really love her. I am hoping she has a black lamb just like her someday.

That first winter, we had a series of blizzard-like storms. They even named the storms. The one that brought the most snow was Ivan. My son trekked down to the stream and woodlands to take pictures. He took hay down for the deer herd in our woodlands. We never lost power, but all the pipes froze. We were using the old well to bring up water for the sheep, bath, and toilet. I heated water on the stove to wash my hair, bathe, and do dishes. It was like being on an endless camping trip, I guess. We used the wood stove and it had to be stocked every two to three hours. Did not get much sleep that winter. At least the sheep had plenty of hay that I supplemented with Alfalfa pellets and Black Sunflower Seeds. We were not prepared for a winter in Maine. It snowed so much I could not tell where the fences were. I had to keep the sheep in because they would walk on top of the crust and go prune the neighbor's lilac bushes. So they had lockdown and in a way, we did too. We could not use the oil heart because the water pipes froze. Winter was well, Maine.

Heart was standing in the pan, banging it with her horns. She was letting me know it was empty and it was time for lunch. I would give the girls snacks at noon when they were young. My phone had alarms that went off for mealtimes for my flock. I swear the sheep knew exactly when the alarm would sound. I would hear Heart ringing in on her feed pan. Glimmer would knock at the door with her horns sometimes too. I think maybe they were spoiled a little.

First winter for my flock. Heart is getting bigger, but still second smallest. Glimmer is the smallest now because she got sick with shipping fever. The trip was hard on her because she was so stressed. Looking back, I should have picked up the ewes the farthest away first and my southern girls last. That way they would have had a lot less time on the road. Glimmer contracted shipping fever from stress. Now that Glimmer is better, she has some catching up to do. Everywhere Heart goes,

Ulfa is there too. They are joined at the hip. Both have leadersheep genetics, and it's self-evident in their inquisitive nature. I loved Heart's goofy way of looking at me. She would often turn her head to one side. So funny, Heart. "Do I look better sideways?"

Heart is on high alert. I wore my raccoon hat outside. No worries, people. Fake fur, no animals were harmed in this confusing moment in time. Heart was staring at my head. I took the hat off and she looked at me then the hat in my hand. She did not approve. So I took the hat back in the house and brought her some cookies. All better now. Hehehe.

Glimmer and Everdeen found the birdseed I put out for the birds. How in the world did they do that? The snow is up to their bellies. They had to go out the side barn door and around to the other side to find the birdseed on top of a sheet of plywood. Those southern girls have a nose for treats, don't they?

White so bright and clean, like new fallen snow glistening against the clear blue sky. Rosy colored clouds and the moon. Beauty seen never seems the same on film, so I take pictures in my mind. Memories to bring forth when I am too old to hike about and seek the mysteries of life. Oh, sweet memories that play back in my heart and mind of journey's past and moments in time. One was when I was sitting on an old burned stump watching the fingers of light touch the valley below. To see the light, play on the waters, and make it shimmer with a life of its own. A moment in time to take your breath away. Beauty so pure and sweet it makes tears come to my eyes. So blessed am I to have a spirit that can be still and wait and watch and behold the beauty all around me.

Pi was my very first ram. I put a deposit down to hold a Ram lamb in 2014, a year before he was born. Kindhorn Farm in Vermont had been recommended by so many people as to where to buy outstanding Ram with excellent bloodlines. "The ram is half your flock; buy the best you can afford," they said.

I watched the posts that Kathy Boulton posted about each ewe and their AI match. Gossie was my favorite ewe and her Icelandic sire (AI) match was Blettur, a gorgeous black and white spotted ram with a regal look. I had two other ewes I put on my list just in case Gossie had all ewe lambs. Gossie had a very square build and lovely udder. Her sire was Dropie, which is one of my favorite Icelandic sires in Iceland. When Gossie lambed, she had twins, a beautiful black-spotted ram lamb and a white-patterned ewe lamb. The moment I saw his picture I knew I had to have him. He had a Pi symbol on his side, and I am an Engineer. Perfect! I had visions of Heart's lambs with him the most. My fellow shepherd, Cathy, wanted a ram lamb from her and Pi.

My son and I went to pick Pi up at Elaine Clark's farm in November. She has some wonderful Icelandics too. She had also purchased a ram from Kindhorn and offered to transport Pi to Maine. When I saw him, I was so impressed. His fleece was immense, and his horns were huge too. They were black with a white stripe.

When we arrived at our farm, we backed up to the side Ell door and opened the back of the truck. The Ell door going out to the barn was closed with the ewes on the other side. Pi *Bah*ed and the ewes answered. Then Pi leaped from the truck into the Ell before Eric could get the ramp in position. He bashed through the half gate into the little Ell and proceeded to chase my little flock of ewes around the pasture for over an hour. *Hm*, so this is what having a Ram is like. Gates need to be much stronger and they don't need ramps to get where they want to go. He is only six months old but is built so well, so strong like a miniature bulldozer. I am so excited to see what the lambs will look like. So glad I waited until the ewes were all over a year old to breed. Now Heart and Glimmer are both huge. Heart is bigger than him too. Heart wasn't sure about my beautiful ram Pi from Kindhorn Farm. She lowered her horns, but he wasn't interested in horns at all. She decided he was okay to stay but didn't like him chasing the ewes around when he first came.

I already have lambs dancing through my brain, and Heart! So excited about Heart's lambs this coming spring. Ewe lambs stay with me. Maybe I will even keep a Ram lamb if I get a Spotted Moorit, oh!

During the winter months I gave my girls kale, spinach, chard, pumpkins, and winter squash. They also ate black sunflower seeds and kelp. When the hay was poor, I fed Alfalfa Pellets to supplement. If you have poor hay, you need to supplement, or they will lose condition. If you feed too much, they get fat and have a hard time lambing. It takes time to learn. The backbone, hips, and ribs should be covered. But you don't want mounds of fat on them either. I had mine too fat one year and there were some problems birthing.

My son hung a kick bag for the sheep to keep them entertained. Faith liked it right away. I used to be able to kick it about midhigh. My son was incredibly good at martial arts and knew several types. We also gave the sheep an old basketball. I tried the cheap, plastic balls from Walmart, but Pi would pop them within a day or two. He loved to bash them in.

The Loss of My Son: My son is no longer in pain

My son chose to take his life yesterday after trying to get medical help for over a year. He was in such agony these last few weeks he would gasp and his face would go white. He had muscle spasms that you could visibly see going through his shoulders, back, and arms. His hands and legs had begun to tingle and go numb at times. It is extremely hard for the uninsured to get medical help if you are a single, white male. For someone with short term memory loss and brain damage, the paperwork and maze of hoops the system puts you through is horrendous. He finally got a social worker counselor that was helping him with paperwork. My son was filling out paperwork to go on disability here at home when he asked me what the Roman Numerals meant on the front page. I said eighteen. He took the papers over to the woodstove and burnt all of them saying three times six is eighteen, it is the mark of the beast. He said he would rather die than take that number.

Yesterday morning, I awakened with a feeling that something was wrong, but I did not know what. I went upstairs into his room to check on him and I never do that. He was not there, and my heart sank. I knew. I walked out to the barn and found him hanging in there. He was lifeless and cold. I screamed and cried, calling out to God in the depth of my pain and sorrow.

Through the anguish I called 911. The people who responded were truly kind. My pastor and friends were there for me in my sorrow and pain to cry with me. God bless all of you who have reached out with sympathy and encouragement. My daughter is on her way now and is taking care of all the arrangements. She is a pillar of strength and comfort to me. My brother and sisters' families have all sent their love. I probably will not respond to all messages but please know I do appreciate your kindness. Please continue to pray for me that no bitterness or unforgiveness takes root in me. Pray that God will give me wisdom in making decisions about the farm. God be with you all.

Poem left by my son. He committed suicide on March 2, 2015. I miss you, my son. My heart is still broken.

VIEWS FROM SPACE

If these were the last words, I spoke to you… Would it be?

Life is what you make it?

Or that it is yet to be seen…

Live each day as if it were your last…

Too proud…too primal…

Too unspoiled some strain to think…

It should be so much easier…

If only I had known what to change.

Riding on this star… That has so many names.

KEENING

From the depths of my soul, the keening began this morning.
I awoke to the revelation that my son is really dead.
It is not some horrendous nightmare that I can wake from,
The very essence of my soul feels as though
it has been wounded beyond repair.
Wailing into the heavens, my cries are
now one with my grieving dog.
Sorrow, the waves of utter dark sorrows
that wash over Angus and me.

March 4, 2015

Angus helped me grieve today. I started crying, almost like a wailing. Angus came over and leaned into me and began to howl. My wailing turned to an eerie howl so wild and free I felt it touch the heavens. Run free, my son, through the Valley and Trees of Heaven that God has created for people like us. I can almost see the smiling face and the presence of two white dogs. One that looks like a wolf and a little dog with a smile and a curled tail.

BRIGHT LIGHT IN THE SKY

Is that you I see smiling back at me tonight?

It's like your face is shining with the glory of God around you.

Such joy, no pain or sorrow.

A spirit set free from the broken body of pain.

I will miss you but I do understand. That you couldn't stay.

I love you and always will, you will always be my only son.

Until we meet again, keep singing songs and save a place for me in your part of heaven.

Filled with conifers and deciduous virgin forests of every kind.

Water Falls and rapids that will blow my mind.

Sunrises and sunsets so beautiful that all you can do is smile with your heart.

Oh, and Eric, say hi to my mom, dad, my brother Jon and my dear little Mackenzie.

Today my son's body will be cremated. My daughter and I will read some letters written to him by my daughter, her husband, Cheyenne, Fletcher, Christine and I. there will be a memorial in California in June for him to give all his family and friends a moment in time to express their love. I will continue to post a poem a day written by him until Easter. We began a fast on Ash Wednesday and I will continue until Easter. The fast is just giving up meat and processed foods. He believed that we all need to pray and fast to purify our body, soul, and spirit. A way to reach a higher place to know the will of God. If my people who are called by my name truly humble themselves, and fast, and pray, then will I hear from heaven and heal their land."

Take a moment today and pray for our country and its people of all cultures and nations.

Poem my son wrote:

SHIRAK

"Gentle as the breeze from the wings of a butterfly...
Antithetical people find they can't map or chart my mind.
Abstract thinking, it's so hard to define...
For a person who only drinks one kind of wine.

Ulfa was my kindred spirit. She would come to me and lay her head in my hand. She knew my heart. I was going through so much that year. My son was very ill, and pain wracked his body. My old Eskie was in failing health too. Mackenzie was fifteen and I just couldn't imagine life without her. Ulfa wasn't the only ewe that gave me love during this time. Everdeen would lay her head on my lap. Heart would cock her head and smile at me. They were my reasons to get up each morning. I spent a lot of time in the barn talking to them.

Bitter cold winds howling outside. The fire is warm inside. I need to spruce up the house for the arrival of my daughter. She is flying out tomorrow to help me with arrangements. Arms to hold in shared sorrow. Good night and sweet dreams. I pray for those who are overwhelmed and feel alone. I pray for those who are in sorrow and pain. May God give you beauty for the ashes at your feet. May he restore your joy and give you peace during your time of mourning. May this year be a year of wondrous blessings from above that put a song of praise upon your lips.

My Ulfa when she found me crying in the barn. She knew my heart was breaking and I saw the concern in her eyes. Ulfa came to me and laid her head against my chest. I wrapped her in my arms and cried and cried. She was there for me through the loss of my son and my sweet fur baby. Sometimes, I think God sends special animals into our lives that are like angels to comfort us in times of sorrow and pain. Ulfa, I will write your story even if it is only for me and memory of a kindred Spirit I loved.

Ulfa smiled at me. I asked her if she knew how much I loved her. Her eyes said yes. Without Ulfa, I do not know how I would have been able to handle the death of my son and my fur baby, Mackenzie.

March 22, 2015

Waves of sorrow rolling over me like the waves of a cold winter sea. Every year I take a selfie on my birthday. This year I really have none I can post that would not show a woman grieving for her only son. They say the eyes are a mirror to the soul. My soul is torn asunder and it will be a long time before I feel the laughter within like the warm summer rain on dry and weary plains. Blessings to all of you that have reached out to me during this time of sorrow and searching.

March 28, 2015

My only son took his life March 2, 2015. Racked by pain, unable to get the medical help he needed, the pain became too much. I am still coping with his loss. My daughter and grandchildren are still healing. If you are thinking of suicide, please talk to someone. People do love you. They will miss you and your life has purpose. You may not see it now, but while there is life there is hope. Reach out, talk to someone. You are loved.

Eyes that show the depth of our pain.

They say that the eyes are a mirror of our soul. Who is this woman looking back at me? The sorrow I see through the facade of a smile. I cut my hair to show the spirit of my grief. Tomorrow, I will smudge sage for you. As they did in ancient days. My heart overflows with memories of you, my son. Until I see you again.

MISSING YOU

In the stillness of the morning light,
I feel your presence near me.
Though holding you would be like holding onto
the mist of the fading shadows light.
Sometimes I hear a heart beating like a cool, clean,
mountain stream rushing against the rocks.
Like a song in the night,
that comes from somewhere in your mind.
Like a memory swept by too fast to hold.
Only a faint-hearted smile within and then it dies,
like a tear that traces down your face.

Until all I hear is the sound of leaves talking
to the winds of change, yet nothing I can see.
If I reach out with my heart and spirit now,
can I grasp the wind?
Can I soar with you above the woodland's canopy and
watch the fingers of light kiss the valley below?
Can I dance in the currents of the wind,
and feel the exhilaration of being swept away?
Wondering if I will be able to break away,
before I plummet back into the chasm of time?
I know that time is just a breath in the mist,
that blends and fades away.
There is nothing left to hold, and my arms are empty now.
And yet still I feel your presence near.
I miss you.

Ulle with her sweet kissy face on. Heart with her smile right behind her. I know I am loved. Icelandic sheep are intelligent, and they have such wonderful personalities. I am so thankful I am a shepherd and I am loved. I have always felt a bit out of place in this world except when I am surrounded by God's creation or animals. I feel their spirits and I believe they know mine. We are connected in some way that is beautiful and pure.

My friend Kathy came over today and looked at the ewes with me. She says Glimmer looks like she will be first. Ulle is humongous, like the triplets' size. Faith is almost as big. Evergreen is getting huge too suddenly. Heart and Ulfa are not showing as much.

Spring 2015 Crackers

I looked out into the pasture and my ewes were busy nibbling on some green grass that had sprouted a patch, where the snow had melted. It looked like Everdeen had a leg stuck on something. I hollered "Hey, are you okay over there?"

An answering Bah from all six ewes and a thundering of many hooves. Oh my goodness, look at those big bellies swaying. Lambies are having the ride of their lives. They all come charging up to the fence to see what I have for them. I have nothing. "Um, just a minute girls, I will find something."

There is a package of soda crackers on the counter. I sneak out with them and toss them to the wind. It's raining crackers and the girls are running around, munching them down as fast as they can. Even Heart has gotten into it. Next time someone has tomato soup, they are going to ask, "Who ate the Crackers?"

"Wasn't me," I will say. Hee-hee

Spring 2015 Crackers

Amanda with the Flock. This little girl has a special way with animals. Sheep, chickens, they all love her. One visitor to the farm I am always happy to see.

April 16, 2015. First ewe to Lamb on Coldstream Icelandic Sheep Farm was Glimmer. I am so thankful that when my son passed away, a gentleman from the Cold Stream State Fishery Department left his number and said if I needed help with lambing to call him. Glimmer was a first-time mom and even though I am a first time Icelandic mom, I knew she was in trouble. She had been in hard labor for an hour. The lamb was stuck and I couldn't figure out what to do.

Fear started to grip my heart when I remembered the offer. I called the Fish Hatchery in a panic, but he was not in the building. The person that answered said he would try to contact him for me. I waited, praying with Glimmer. I heard a truck pull up and called out to him.

He checked Glimmer out and said the lamb's front legs were not in the correct position. He pulled one leg at a time forward. Even in the correct position, a rope was needed because her head was swollen. The lamb was large, and Glimmer was my smallest ewe. I asked him if the lamb was dead and he said no, her tongue is moving. He pulled with Glimmer's contractions and a beautiful Mouflon ewe lamb was born. She weighed 9.6. No wonder Glimmer had trouble.

Glimmer cleaned with vigor but did butt her lightly a few times. She was probably telling her she didn't like the long, painful labor. When she butted her, it scared me though. I almost took her away. So glad I didn't. Glimmer was very protective; she stomped her foot at Heart when she came to see the lamb. The next morning, I found a pile of feathers, with what was left of Grumpy, Red Hen. Glimmer had pounded her into the ground. I am going to make sure Dumdum stays on the other side of the fence. I named Glimmer's lamb Finni, in honor of the Fish Hatchery that saved her life. Brought her in the house to weigh her. She is strong and bold like her mom.

Faith was the next to lamb and she had no trouble. The first one born was a tiny little black ewe with frosted lips and ears. Almost immediately, a brown (moorit) ram lamb was born. He was stillborn though, and nothing I did could bring him to life. Then much to my surprise, another black ram lamb appeared. He had frosted lips, ears, and a flash of frosted silver on each side. The little ewe lamb was so tiny, 3.8 pounds. It was bitter cold, -17 degrees that day and the lambs chilled quickly. I think the lambs might have been born early. Faith cleaned them and talked to them, but their sucking reflexes were very weak. I tried holding them up to nurse but Faith wouldn't hold still for them. She accidentally stepped on the ram lamb and damaged his knee. So I gave up, wrapped a towel around them, and took them in the house to warm up. I used the hair dryer and then gave them a warm enema to bring up their core temperature like Elaine had recommended. Then I milked Faith's rich colostrum into a bottle.

After they drank some milk and were warmed up, I took them back out to try again. Faith was attentive but wouldn't stand still for them to nurse. I decided to bottle feed. Looking back now, I wish I had tried harder to get them on their mom. She wanted them. I was sick with pneumonia and just couldn't handle it alone.

Peeri was so tiny. I named her Peeri, which means Fairy. She is such a dainty little thing with those slender black legs and darling little nose. The inside of her ears was silvery, and her lips were frosted like she dipped them in sugar.

Her brother, we called Flash.

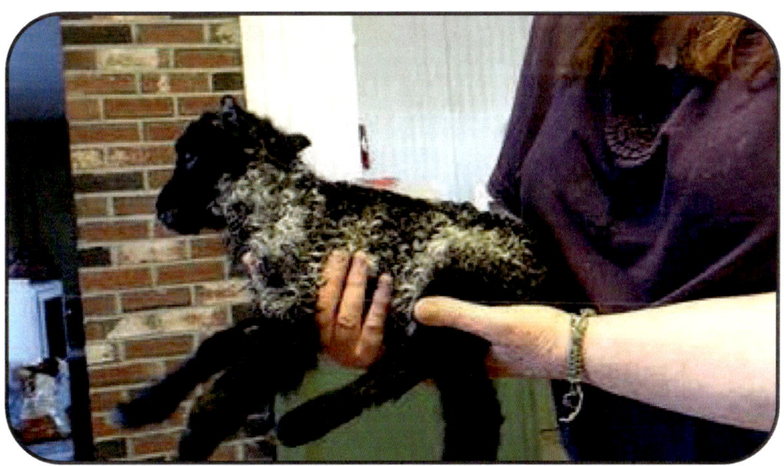

He had a Flash of silver on his sides. He also had the sugar lips. He was bigger and stronger than Peeri, weighing in at 4.9. He wouldn't stay in the crate and would jump out within a few minutes. He was also the first to climb on the couch, so we started putting nappies on him and his sister. They stayed in the house until they were about a month old and we put them in the dog run. It had an igloo doghouse that was plenty big enough for them. They could also see the flock and get used to other sheep. After an introductory time, the lambs were allowed in with the main flock. At mealtime I would just say, "Come here babies," and they would come running. Heart watched over them when they joined the flock.

There were no lambs for Heart that first year of lambing. I could see the love and longing in her eyes for a lamb of her own. She would lay beside the bottle lambs and watch them play or sleep. Once when she was standing next to them, Peeri started looking for milk. Heart had no udder, so no milk for Peeri. Heart had a big smile on her face though. "Yeah, shepherd. They love me, don't they?" She watched over every lamb born and was the first one to respond if a lost lamb cried out. After the bottle lambs joined the flock, she watched over and protected them in the meadows.

Jeanie Fennel, my Pastor's wife and I took Peeri to Cummings Senior Facility. Everyone loved her and she was really a hit. Peeri had to wear a nappy and she tried to bounce out of it a few times. The seniors really enjoyed the show she put on and clapped their hands. They thought she was showing off for them, maybe she was. Jeanie Fennel and I took Peeri around to some of the rooms to visit a few more people. After her bottle, she fell asleep in my arms and there was no waking her. Una even tried giving her a kiss on the nose, but it was for naught. She slept for over an hour.

Flash had a crooked leg after Faith stepped on him. It never straightened out all the way. I was hoping it would. I tried a piece of foam pipe insulation over some cotton wrap for a while, but I don't think I left it on long enough. They had nappies on here, so they are ready for a visit.

Ram lambs have different personalities than ewe lambs. At an early age, they are more aggressive and like to butt other lambs, people, and just about anything. I have a soccer ball for my lambs to play with. Never play by encouraging them to butt you. It may be cute or fun when they weigh twenty pounds, but it won't be when they weigh two hundred pounds. Many ram lambs raised on bottles end up going to freezer camp because of this. If you have a ram lamb, you can have him neutered and made into a fiber wether. They have a calmer disposition and give you beautiful fleece twice a year.

Peeri visited the Ammadarmast Grange #379, Enfield for the 4-H Fiber Event. A darling little girl bottle fed her while we were there. I think it was Mike and Missy's daughter. Peeri had a little harness on and people could take her for walks. Peeri's brother had to stay home. He was bigger and much more RAMbunctious.

I try and support 4-H and FFA as much as I can. Children need to get involved with farm animals and learn about caring for them. With Icelandics, there is so much more than just raising for meat. They can raise them for their beautiful fleeces. Then learn to shear, clean the fleeces, card them, spin to make yarn, and finally, either felt, weave, or knit.

I love sharing the Viking sheep story with people of all ages. Most people don't know the Viking sails and tent-like shelter were made of woven wool. They also made their clothing, blankets, and hats from wool. The horns were used for drinking vessels, storage and many other things. The Viking sheep were also milked for their rich, creamy milk that made wonderful cheese.

Icelandics are the perfect sheep for a homesteader. They brose brush and are easy keepers. The milk is high in butterfat and makes great butter or cheese. They are smaller than the huge meat breeds, but the lambs grow very fast and are ready to butcher within seven months. The fabulous fleeces come in so many shades of autumn and gray. Perfect for those who love to work with natural colors. They do come in white pattern too, if you like to dye. The light greys make for a lovely over dye. What I love the most about Icelandics is their intelligence and unique personalities.

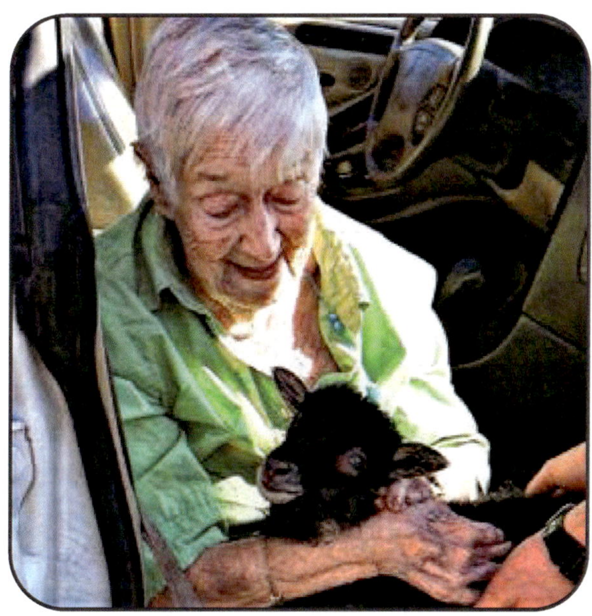

We also had driven by visits for people with mobility issues. We would bring Peeri out for a visit with them. Sometimes they would help with a bottle. Liv fed her a bottle one day and Una dropped by for a visit a few days later. Watching the ladies made my heart smile. We also had some young adults with forms of Autism visit out farm. Animals are so therapeutic for just about anyone. Who wouldn't love to hold a fluffy lamb?

The lambs also visited a Church and a School by request. There is educational material you can share with the lambs about the Vikings, or they can just be therapeutic. One school we visited, there were a couple of boys who started telling me about the plants, roots, and bugs the Vikings dyed their wool with. Turns out, their family is active in Historic Events depicting the ancient ways. What a wonderful way to learn history and culture.

I have noticed a new awakening of the vintage crafts and history. Many young people learning about weaving on a loom, spinning yarn, dyeing materials, and using roots and flowers for the dye. It warms my heart to see this happening. So much will be lost if we don't pass these skills onto the youth. I remember standing by my grandmother as she canned, shelled peas, cut and wrapped meat, knitted, sewed clothing, and did beautiful embroidery. How I wish I had been able to retain more of what I was taught. I was truly blessed to have both sets of grandparents when I was young. One set on the Ocean where I learned how to dig clams, fish, smelt, and make chowder. The other set in Ohio farmland where I learned so many things it would take another book to tell. Many stories of our heritage are passed down through the grandparents' sharing. It is so important. I have so many memories to share because of them.

March 2015. Ulle was the third ewe to lamb on Coldstream Icelandic Sheep Farm. Poor Ulle had a very rough birth too. Her huge ewe lamb was over ten pounds. The lamb was stuck, Ulle was groaning, and I was in tears. I called out in my anguish "Lord I can't do this, why is everything so hard?"

Then I heard "You can do it Cheri, she needs you, don't give up." Confused, I looked toward the sound of the voice.

It was my neighbor Janet. She had walked down from her senior housing because she just knew I needed her. I took a deep breath and said, "Help me, help Ulle. Lord, give us a live lamb, please."

I took a little towel and grabbed one foot and pulled. Then the other foot, like I had seen the Fish Hatchery man do. Oh, thank God, something released. Must have been her elbows. I pulled down and slightly turned as the lamb came like he had done with Finni. She was alive, and the color of baby poo. Yuck, a brownish orange lamb. Found out later the color was because she was stressed during birth. Ulle was exhausted and so was I.

Heart came over to check us all out. I stroked her nose. "Maybe next year for you sweetie, just try and have two small lambs instead of one humongous one." Then I heard Janet laugh. I had forgotten she was there for a moment. I am so thankful for my friends.

A problem developed though. Ulle wouldn't let Rapunzel nurse unless I tied her and pushed her up against the wall. She was sniffing my pocket the next day while I had her pinned. Must be the Life Savers she smells. I said, "Be nice to your lamb and you'll get more of these. She loved the Life Savers. Every time I went in to push her up against the wall so Rapunzel could nurse, I gave her a Life Saver. After a while she would go up against the wall when she saw me come. Then I caught her nursing without a Life Saver. Hahaha. Ulle, I caught you. I gave her a Life Saver anyway.

Ulle was an excellent mom after she had the whole mother thing figured out. I think when the birth is traumatic it takes them a bit longer to bond. I called Ulle's lamb Rapunzel because of her long curls. Later I changed it to Drifa, which means Snow in Icelandic. She was such a beautiful lamb. I boasted she would be my show winner. I never showed her, but the young man in 4-H did, and I gifted her too.

I brought Rapunzel in to weigh her and put her down by the bottle lambs. Flash came over to see what she was. She is so much bigger than the triplets. She weighs more than Flash and Peeri combined and she is younger. Amazing how long Rapunzel's fleece is. Peeri and Flash have soft, short curls.

Everdeen was nesting, singing her mother's song to her lambs. Every ewe has her own song and that is how they imprint onto their lambs. At least that is my take on it. She was nesting (walking around, digging in the bedding, laying down, walking) and digging for a while now. Finally, she laid down and started to push. I saw one white leg and one black leg coming so at first, I thought it might be two lambs, but it wasn't. She delivered a beautiful black ewe lamb with high white socks and a white collar.

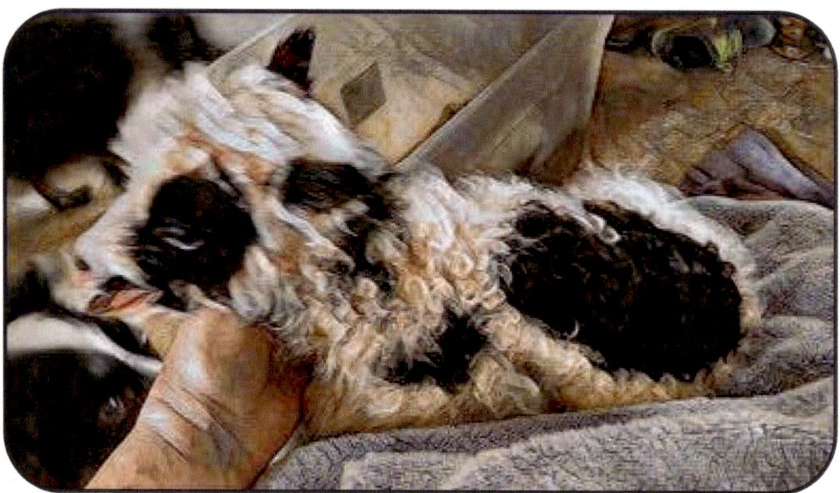

The next lamb presented with only one leg, so I checked and found one front leg bent at the knee. I pushed the one leg back a bit so I could reposition the other. This one was a tiny ram lamb with black on his back and face. Everdeen was talking to her lambs and licking them. I waited until both lambs suckled then went to bed. At lamb check, I found the little ram lifeless under a pole. My helper had propped a pole against the gate to make sure it stayed shut. Sometime during the night, it fell over and landed on the little ram. I thought he was dead but after lifting him up he made a feeble cry. I ran into the kitchen with him and checked him for broken bones. I know he needed to warm up fast, so I checked with my shepherd friends and was told to give him a warm enema. It would bring his core temperature up. Then put him in a sink full of warm water. That did the trick. He was revived enough to lift his little head. Thinking he was probably hungry, I made him a bottle of Colostrum replacement. He drank a few ounces. After I brought Evan's core temperature up and gave him colostrum replacement, I tried to reintroduce him to Everdeen. She wanted nothing to do with him.

I found out later that putting him in the warm water in the sink probably washed off the scent she needed to bond with him. You're supposed to put the lamb in a plastic bag with its head out and float him in the warm water. Now I know. I already had two lambs that I was bottle-feeding and was totally overwhelmed. When my friend Cathy offered to raise him, I was overjoyed to send him off to her loving arms. Cathy had children that were excited to help bottle feed. Their golden dog Chloe decided to take him under her wings, her paws, and her bed became his bed too. He slept in her bed with her and it was hard to tell where the lamb ended and she began. He did take up some doggy habits though, like chasing cars and playing with a ball.

Katniss was my favorite lamb that year. She had a ruffle of white around her neck like a lace collar. Her fleece had tons of very long curls and she had three white socks and a crown of white. She was a momma's girl and stayed very close to Everdeen. Everdeen was a very protective mother and watched over her diligently.

Life can go from happy dance to sobs of grief in but a moment I found Katniss wedged between the feeder and the fence. She had her head pinned back and was lifeless. Her mother Everdeen was standing beside her, looking at me to make everything right. No sign of injury, no froth on her lips. She was a healthy weight, even a bit chubby with a beautiful full fleece of curls. I screamed in anguish of heart and spirit. My grandson comes running and sees me sobbing over Katniss. He drops down on his knees and wraps his arms around me, crying too. "What happened Nana?"

I explained how I found her. He put Katniss on a tarp and carried her away. Everdeen watches him go then looks at me. She stares at me with those big brown liquid eyes full of pain and sorrow. Then she turns away and walks to the corner of the barn pressing her head against the wall. Then she laid down with her head facing into the dark corner. I sat next to her and talked to her, but she turned her head away. My heart is broken. She blames me. As I am crying, I post my grief, feeling like I have failed. My sheep deserved better on Facebook. People encouraged me and told me that sheep seem to look for ways to die or get injured. One person says I must be bipolar.

My post was: "My heart is broken, and I am rehoming all my sheep. They need a better shepherdess."

After I posted that, I received so much encouragement to carry on with the farm, not to give up. It's been so hard losing my dog, then my only son, now my favorite ewe lamb. I just don't understand why, sometimes.

I was thinking to myself, I really need to stabilize, don't I? I do have a deep, abiding faith in God. It's just so hard sometimes. Death is not something I deal with very well. No second chance. Poof, they are gone and the pain cuts like a knife. I have always been empathetic even as a child. Maybe I am bipolar? Does that make me any less of a person? I am who I am. I can't pretend that everything is okay when I feel shredded. I am not perfect and never will be. So strange how the ones we love so much can leave us so quickly. It hurts.

Then I realized that I was not alone during this traumatic event. My grandson was here, and we grieved together. He comforted me and then carried Katniss away. He buried her deep in the ground while the summer sun beat down on him. I am thankful for my grandson. When we buried Katniss today, I didn't even think about her pelt or fleece. Some people ask me if we kept her fleece. It never crossed my mind to shave her. I don't think I could have done it anyway.

She was more of a fluffy snuggle pet than a sheep. Maybe I will get tougher as time goes on or maybe I won't. Grief is heavy on my heart and I know I need to spend time with the Creator. After driving for a few miles, I walk to the riverbank and sit still, waiting in one of my favorite places. It is a beautiful, peaceful place with a big mossy rock to sit on. I love to watch the light play on the waters. Breathing in the sweet, clean air, I bow my head and heart to pray. I seek the only one who can give me the inner peace I need. It's been too long since I have done this. I know I have been caught up in the business of life and death. Forgive me, Father and renew my Spirit this day. As I wait, the leaves begin to dance as if the breath of the Spirit moves through them. Gently, Lord you speak to my heart and mind. My dream is not to end with the death of Katniss. She was much loved and had a wonderful mother. Her life was short but very happy. We are not promised that nothing will ever go wrong once we know you. We are promised you will never leave or forsake us. "Create in me a clean heart and renew a right spirit in me. Give me strength to walk each day according to your will and be thankful for the blessings, Amen."

I look at the tree anchored on the rock and remember I am to do the same. Even when the water is high and flowing fast, the tree remains. Keep me grounded Lord, give me that peace that passes all understanding during the storms of life. Help me focus on the good and not dwell on sorrows of the past. Give my heart hope and joy in the future. Amen.

April 2015. Ulfa was the only one that just surprised me with twin lambs. They were up dry and nursing when I went out to check the jugs. The ewe lamb looked just like Ulfa. The ram lamb was so gorgeous. He was a single gene grey Mouflon Spotted. So colorful, with lots of white spotting patterns and then patches of shades of grey, tan, and black. I named the ewe lamb Athena. She is Ulfa's mini me. Apollo was trying to get out of the jug (a jug is a small fenced area used to bond with lambs) to explore the same day he was born. Athena was a mommy's girl and liked to snuggle up with her mom. I usually keep the ewes and lambs in a large jug for three days then let them out with the others. When I opened Ulfa's jug, she bolted out without the lambs. She ran over to each ewe in the flock and butted them once, except Heart. Then she ran back and brought her lambs out of the jug. Everyone stayed clear of her. She was reminding everyone she was still in charge and not to mess with her lambs. Hahaha. Athena is now Surtsie and is on Trinity Farm. She is Ulfa's beautiful legacy.

April 2015. Ulfa's beautiful ram lamb Apollo. He was so inquisitive like his mom as a lamb. When Roxy the farm dog came over to the gate, he was sticking his head through to check her out. Heart loved this adventuresome lamb. Visitors often thought he was her lamb because they spent so much time together. Apollo was and still is my favorite ram lamb born on Coldstream Ice. You could see intelligence in his eyes. He was stunning I loved his striped horns and hooves. He was perfect in my eyes. I was hoping Ulfa would have a ewe lamb next year that looked just like him. So Pi would have to be her flock sire again this Fall.

March 16, 2015

There is a place that I can go within the woodland's filtered light. A mossy rock there waits for me. Around it there are many ferns that stand in dappled light. I hear the rushing, clean stream nearby. The air is sweet with the scent of Pine. My refugee from the insanities of the outside life.

Sept 2015.

Athena went on to Trinity Farms and became a member of their flock. She had such a beautiful face and fleece. I knew she was something very special. So thankful she had an exceptional Farm to go to. I knew Margarete Flowers would take good care of her. She raised some fabulous Leadersheep and had all the Leadersheep Lines represented in her flock.

There is a couple of great educational videos on YouTube that are about Leadersheep in Iceland. Leadersheep are a separate lineage within the Icelandic breed. They are more intelligent than other sheep and the other sheep follow them. They are know when blizzards are coming and lead their flocks to safety ahead of storms.

Sept 2015.

First Lamb Crop 2015. My first lamb crop playing in the field. Faith's twins are in the small meadow with Heart. I only had five first time ewes lamb this year. The lambs are so colorful. Black and white, white pattern, SGGM, SGGM spotted, black Mouflon, and the two Black grays with Heart. Such a variety and all healthy. I am very blessed.

White Pattern is not white; it is a pattern that masks whatever color the sheep is. A seemingly white sheep might really be black or (moorit) brown. Icelandic sheep only come in two base colors— black and brown— but the shades of brown with the grey pattern make many variations of those colors. White patterned sheep can have black or brown lambs. You need at least one white patterned parent to have a white lamb. The color genetics of Icelandic sheep is exciting and sometimes confusing. There are six patterns and two colors. Oh, and the spotting. Lambing is a fun time of year. Waiting to see what color and pattern the lambs will be. Black is a dominant color over brown most of the time. Unless the black sheep has one brown parent.

Cleaned the pastures of anything I thought would be a danger to the lambs. Moved to the corner. Where do I see all the lambs gather? Yeah, you got it.

Lamb shade:

Wow. Talk about excitement. I heard the thunder of many feet charging downstairs and across the house amid some words that are not allowed plus one word that gripped my heart. "Lamb!" Boots were jammed on feet. Some on wrong feet and out the house into the pasture dashed my daughter, granddaughter, grandson, and Josh. I looked to where they were headed not knowing what carnage I would see. What an odd sight, a lamb walking with the heat lamp on her head minus the bulb, like a garish hat. Two people lifted her up and the other two worked on a gentle release. After they checked her over, she was set down. She shook her little head and bounced off to see what else she could find to get into.

I went outside with my son's old sandals one morning and Heart was curious as to where he was. She could smell him there, but the feet were mine. I went out once with his slippers into the field and the whole flock surrounded me. They were smelling my feet. I think they missed him and couldn't figure out where he was. He spent a lot of time in the barn sitting in the hammock chair with the small door open. There was a wonderful view of the woodlands and meadows. It was a great place to watch the sunset too. Job, his cat, would lay in his lap and the sheep would bed down around him. I know they loved him.

October 2015. My white hen Guinevere hopped into the pasture with the sheep, to check out the pumpkins. Heart lowered her head at the intruder and took a couple of steps toward her. Guinevere her to bring him over. Oh, my goodness that sweet little face. I cupped his little chin and looked into proceeded to fly up onto Hearts' back. All the ewes looked at Heart in amazement, what would she his eyes. Then I checked his eye membranes. White. They were alabaster white. "Oh no, Cathy he is do? Heart decided to ignore the chicken on her back and maybe it would go away. Guinevere hopped dying of a worm load." down and started eating pumpkin seeds. All the ewes took Heart's clue and ignored her too.

Fall 2015. Guess who's back? Evan is seven months old and he is way too tiny to use for breeding. Cathy called and said she didn't think she could use Evan for breeding because he was so small. I told her to bring him over. Oh, my goodness that sweet little face. I cupped his little chin and looked into his eyes. Then I checked his eye membranes. White. They were alabaster white. "Oh no, Cathy he is dying of a worm load."

She said, "I am so sorry, I didn't know." So we wormed him, gave him some Red Cell, a shot of vitamin B, and some Selenium E. His recovery took a few weeks, but he got stronger every day. I told Cathy she could bring her ewes to my farm for the breeding season. She brought her three ewes over after they were wormed. At thirty pounds, Evan would not be able to be the flock sire. I am wondering if he might be a miniature. I put him in the dog run and he claimed the igloo for himself. What an adorable little ram.

2015

Evan was being so frisky and silly today, like a little lamb. He was hopping around and jumping up on his hind legs too. Then he went over to the fence and lowered his little head and shook his tiny little horns at Glimmer on the other side. Well, she responded with a big blam into the chain link fence. Evan jumped and ran around the corner, peeked then came back, made a face at her, and lowered his little head again. Hahaha you got it, blam again. He is lucky she can't get in with him because she would probably pound him into the ground. Nobody messes with the Glim!

The Glim 2015. Nobody messes with the Glim. Glimmer was so tiny two years ago, but she always had a warrior princess heart. Everdeen had to have stitches in her lip and nose after she got bitten by a dog. Glimmer stood beside the table and watched the veterinarian stitching Everdeen up. She kept stomping her foot at him. He said, "Feisty little ewe, isn't she? Good thing she is not a 2000pound bull."

"Hahahaha. Yeah, that's for sure," I said.

Fall 2015

November 4, 2015

My hay arrived and whoops, there is some Burdock in it. I will have to check it over as I feed. Already have four sheep with burdock and they are going to be sheared.

My shearer did a great job on my sheep. I decided to shear Ulfa. She wasn't as thin as I thought. It's just that the others are so plump. I had six fleeces in a row in the small elle to bag up. While we were in with the small group, Glimmer broke into the elle and ran back and forth through the fleeces. I am so sick about it. They were all sold. I will have to see what I can salvage. I have Everdeen's, Finbar's, Finni's, Drifa's, Ulfa's and Pi's that did not get run over. My best fleeces, Glimmer, Ulle, Faith, and Heart will take some sorting and lots of picking. Would someone like to buy Houdini? I told her she was that close from being dinner.

Amanda, Brittany, and her brother are helping with halter training the lambs. It is hysterical. Drifa face planted on purpose and played dead so Amanda was trying to bribe her with animal cookies. Finni did the dead sheep routine too. Do they talk to each other like, "Hey, let's play dead maybe they will leave us alone."

Finni finally started walking with Brittany. When the other lambs saw, they soon followed suit. So nice to have all the great help training the lambs. Lambs that are handled from birth are so much easier to medicate, worm, and milk when they are old enough.

Fall 2015

Glimmer broke a horn today getting stuck in the fence. I bought some blue cote to put on it. As I was trying to put it on Glimmer's horn, Ulle thought it was a treat and knocked it out of my hand. vI have pinto sheep and blue fingers now. I give myself a fail for this.

Whenever Amanda would come to visit me, she spent a lot of time with the sheep. They were comfortable with her and would line up for scratches. Sometimes she would knock Apples off the tree for them.

Monday

Glimmer got her head stuck again. It took three of us to get her horns out this time. I need a different feeder.

We almost lost Glimmer today. She had her head stuck in the hog wire again. Both horns and her head through. She was hot and sweaty, choking a little. Fletcher found her. I was able to twist her head and get one horn out, then the other. She shook her head and trotted over to the water. Poor girl. I do not know how long she was like that.

Everdeen with her beautiful full fleece. I had a visitor that came to my farm just after Everdeen was sheared the second fall. He asked me if I had any black fleece. I brought out two boxes and I swear he almost fainted. "Ohh, this is every grease spinner's dream," he said. I looked confused, I guess, because he then explained what grease spinning was and why her fleece was perfect for it. I sold him both of Everdeen's fleeces and still wonder to this day what he made from them.

Monday

Heart and Job 2015. Heart loved my son's cat. Job. She would play with his tail and he would pat her nose. After my son passed away, Job left. He missed my son. Eric used to sit in the rope hammock chair in the barn. Job would sit in his lap, purring like a motorboat. I didn't spend enough time with him after my son passed, so he went to live with the neighbors. There was a girl there that liked to pet him, and Job liked the attention.

Photo by Jean Fennel and modified by me.

May 2015. My grandson Fletcher came from California to stay with me after my son passed away. He had been living on the streets and had been in and out of trouble most of his teenage years. When he came to the farm, he was full of anger, sorrow, and pain. I watched this tough gangster kid gradually calm down and become a gentle, caring yet strong young man. When I went to California for my son's memorial, Fletcher took care of our Farm in Maine. He bottle-fed the lambs and got really attached to them. The lambs thrived under his care and they loved their papa.

Fall 2015. When I got back from California after my son's memorial, I saw how much the lambs had grown. That fall, I found someone who wanted to use Flash now (Jarn) for their flock sire. Fletcher had been so worried someone would eat him. Even so, it was hard for him to say goodbye to Jarn. He poured some sweet feed on the grass and sat down with him for a while. Jarn did enjoy his new farm once he got there and saw his flock of lovely ewes. I was so thankful to find homes for all my ram lambs that first year.

In 2015 Heart was so beautiful; everyone wanted a lamb of hers. I couldn't understand why she didn't have any lambs. I finally had a veterinarian check her in 2017 and found out she had ambiguous gender. She would never be able to have her own lambs. I felt terrible that I had been expecting her to lamb each year. There was a reason why she never lambed. It wasn't because she didn't want lambs, she loved lambs. I took her off the breeding list that day and gave her a new title she deserved so well. Heart the Leadersheep: protector of all things small. She chased a fox out of the field once that got in with the lambs.

She was there when each lamb was born. She watched over them and they loved her. She may not be able to have a lamb, but she was Nanny of them all.

September 2015. Ulfa was suffering from some unknown illness. We had several Veterinarians examine her and they did blood work and fecal. The blood work came back normal except for anemia. I started her on Vitamin B12 supplement with Iron. As Ulfa got sicker and weaker Heart took over more of her Leadersheep duties. She lay in the entry every night watching over her flock. I separate the ram lambs in September that year and put them in the dog run with a shelter of their own. Heart insisted on staying out all night and laid between the barn door and the ram lambs' little shed. That way she could watch over both the ram lambs and the rest of her flock. My fellow shepherd, Brittany, saw her laying in the pasture one morning and asked me if she was okay. I explained how the ram lambs were in the dog run and Heart wouldn't leave them at night.

Pictures in my mind.

I take pictures in my mind, soul, and spirit to hold onto when I am very old. I started as a child of six, sitting in a tire swing that was attached to an ancient tree. We were moving that day and I thought to myself, "I need to remember this place with the big red barn and the meadows where the Wildflowers grow." So I reached out with everything I had and drew it into who I am. So one day when I am very old, I could see it again and warm my heart with memories that make me smile. And so it goes.

When I look on this beauty that surrounds me every day of my life, I am overwhelmed with joy. So thankful I have been given a spirit that embraces all I see and hear with my heart.

My heart still aches with sorrow. When will this pain and grieving go away? I know you're happy now and there is no more pain or sorrow but still, the sorrow wells up in me and grabs hold of my heart, makes it hard to breathe. Tears fall silently, and I mourn again for you. Healing will come someday, and my wounded spirit will once again be whole. I miss you, my son.

Oct 12, 2015. My Agricultural student Brittany has been working off a beautiful ewe lamb. She has done an excellent job halter breaker her and training her to lead and stand. Finni was our farm's first lamb. I am so pleased she chose her. Finni is an excellent start for her foundation flock.

I am so thankful for Brittany's hard work on my farm. Not only her help on the farm, but her words of wisdom and comfort. So young, but so wise in the Lord. We spend time in prayer together and our fellowship is sweet. She loves the flock and takes excellent care of them. Her dream is to have her own farm someday and Finni was her first ewe. A good foundation for her beginnings. Next Spring, she can work off another lamb. I love seeing her generation taking up agriculture. They are our future in farming.

Nov 22, 2015 Pi resting his head on the wood chunk. I am going to miss this beautiful ram. I have decided to sell my big ram Kindhorn Airam Pi. I used him for two fall breeding seasons, and it was time for someone with a bigger flock to use his fantastic genetics. His lambs are gorgeous. I only had five ewes and there was a huge single black Mouflon ewe lamb from white patterned Glimmer, a huge white patterned ewe lamb from White Patterned Ulle, Triplets from black Gray Faith. She had two black grays, a ram and ewe that lived, and one Moorit gray that was still born. Everdeen, my black ewe, had two black-spotted lambs, an ewe and a ram. Then there was Ulfa, my SGGM. She had a SGGM ewe lamb and a SGGM Spotted Ram.

I have bred Pi to five ewes again this year. The only difference is Everdeen is in with Finbar and Heart, my Moorit and White Spotted is in with Pi. If she has a Moorit Spotted Ram lamb, I might keep him. Pi really deserves a bigger flock. I believe this Ram is exceptional, one in a million, as far as I am concerned. Kind Horn Farm raises some of the best Icelandic's in North America and I am proud to have owned him. Pi ended up on Fence Row Farm with Marti Favre. He could not have a better home.

Our Farm needed a polled ram and Trista Haggerty contacted me to ask if I would like a black grey Polled ram named Finbar. I looked at his picture and smiled. He is perfect. Finbar was gifted to me by Trista Haggerty of Hawk Circle Wilderness Education and Earth Mentoring Institution. Finbar will have my only polled ewe Everdeen and the two young ewes born this spring. Finbar has an extremely sweet disposition and is gentle with my young ewes. He has a dainty head, so I am hoping the lambs will have smaller heads and there will be easier births for the first-time moms. So Finbar will have white patterned Drifa, black grey Peeri, black Mouflon Finni, and my sweet Everdeen.

Finbar arrived in the car munching on hay. He and the car smell like lavender, courtesy of his home farm. He has a wreath of flowers and herbs on his head. Fletcher looks at him and says he is big and beautiful with a thick, gray, wavy fleece. He said he is going to call him Ziggy. Hmmm, but Fletcher. his name is Finbar. We already have a Zappa-Pi. I am thinking I will let him with his girls a week sooner than Pi. That way, I will have a breather in between the first-time moms and the older ewes.

Finbar's sire is a Moorit grey. His mother is a beautiful black spotted ewe, named Chardonal. He has a fabulous fleece and came with a wreath of herbs on his head. I put Finbar in with the daughters of Pi, Drifa,

Peeri, Finni, and my sweet Everdeen. He chased the little ewes around a while, but Everdeen put a stop to it. They all ran to hide behind her. She shook her polled head at Finbar. "You behave," she seemed to say.

Finbar keeps his three yearling ewes in line. They started butting each other and he stepped in between them. He is our peacekeeper. I wonder where he learned that. Today I gave them graham cracker snacks. I tossed one to Ziggy and he picked it up. One of his girls grabbed a piece of it. He started to lower his head to butt, then raised his head, backed away and let her eat it. What a gentle ram. Maybe polled rams are not as rambunctious as the horned ones.

December 2015. My grandson brought home three orphaned kittens. Skinny and sick with eye infections. I was not sure if they were going to make it. I bathed each one of them. The little black and white spotted one might have a sore nose. I tried to wash one of her spots off her face bye mistake. They loved the old sweater I gave them to snuggle in. My granddaughters were over the moon when they saw them.

My daughter and granddaughters moved from California to Maine in December so they could help me on the farm. It was good to have family around me again. Christmas is drawing near. As memories flood my mind and heart, I am sometimes brought to tears. Missing loved ones no longer with us. Then my granddaughter started singing in the kitchen. She is making spaghetti Cabrera while dancing to Louis Armstrong and Ettinger. Now, here is a heart smile memory.

We have the kittens now and my dogs watch over them. All you have to say is "Where are the babies?" Angus and Roxy will take you to each one.

After medication and a week of love and food they are fat, happy, kittens. Somebody loves them and they are part of our family now. We named the grey one Scoobie Do and the white and black one Ninja. They are both females so I will make sure to get them spayed as soon as I can. It is the responsible thing to do.

The last few days has passed with much joy within my home. Watching my grandgirls play in the snow. Snowball fights, snowmen, and snow angels. I have had some moments of sorrow too. This is my first Thanksgiving and Christmas without my son. He would have been so happy to see his sister and her children here. He was so worried about them living so close to the Border in California. Keep us in prayer. Jennifer will be interviewing for a position in Bangor. The girls need to get enrolled in school. Chey must choose where she will be taking her dance Classes. Pray the transition goes smoothly and they feel at home with their new teachers and classmates. Pray for me too that I can roll with the new flow and be a positive impact on my family. Health for my flock, kids, sheep. and me. Hehe.

Cheyenne and the snow lady.

Christine and the snow lady.

First winter in Maine for the California girl with the exuberate spirit.

Dec 2015. "Hey Heart, aren't you coming in the barn tonight?" Heart smiles but doesn't budge. I hear a bah in the darkness. Oh my, here comes Everdeen and Finni. No wonder you wouldn't let me lock up. "What would I do without you, Heart?" She smiles.

Heart the Leadersheep, watching the new year come in. So Thankful to have my daughter and her three children with me. I wonder what 2016 will bring. What will the lambs look like, the colors and patterns? Will the year be full of sorrow or joy? Probably some of both. I think when we have difficulties, we appreciate the mountain tops so much more. No matter what, as for me and my house we shall serve the Lord.

PROLOGUE INTO
A NEW YEAR

I write poetry when it flows out to express the feelings within. Sometimes memories of long ago. I have always been different, unique in spirit. Something so different I really didn't fit in with is what the world has classified as normal. But that's okay, I am as God intended. I have found peace in who I am and there is a plan and purpose for my life now. It brings laughter to my Spirit and Fulfillment to my soul. I am a shepherd and I am loved.

ONLY ME

I am only me; my name is? I am only me. Why am I only me? Was it because I was an inconvenience to your life? Or a disappointment somehow? Have I always been sitting outside the fishbowl, watching the others swim in a school, a pod, a gathering, a family? But I am only me, I walked a different path. I listened for beautiful sounds that soothe my soul and saw the beauty of God's creation. I loved walking Woodland trails where all you could hear were the songs of birds and the wind talking through the trees. When I tried to walk the paved path with the annoyingly loud, scrambled sounds all around made my spirit sick. I needed my bare feet on the soft green grass. Am I strange to sit still on the warm breathing earth and feel the presence and peace I love? To see the textures of bark on the trees and marvel at the diversity of all the shades of green. I was the crazy girl who spent hours alone staring into the sky at clouds while everyone else got high. I wondered why anyone would want to poison their spirit with mind altering drugs. I would rather sit on a large mossy Rock near the waterfall surrounded by mist, than go to a party where everyone wears a facade. I preferred the company of creatures like horses, cats, and dogs. Now that I am older and wiser, more settled inside, I have found that I love the company of sheep. They listen without judgment and follow you around, burping with pleasure when they get treats. But then that's only me and now my name is shepherd. In that, there is peace.

ABOUT THE AUTHOR

Cheri Magnuson is Shepherd of Coldstream Icelandic Sheep in the beautiful State of Maine. She retired from Aerospace Engineering in 2013 and purchased a small farm in Maine to follow a childhood dream. Since she was a young girl her dream was to someday own a little farm with a clear, clean rushing stream running through it. There would be a healthy woodland full of all kinds of beautiful trees. The most important part of the dream was the lovely meadows where wildflowers grow and a flock of beautiful, colorful sheep. Her dream has become a reality, the journey has been one full of both joy and sorrow. The year her first lambs were born her only son took his life. She found that writing eased the pain and gave her a more positive focus. Writing stirred up a God given gift and gave her a more meaningful existence. So now she shares her dream, the journey of life, on her farm with others. Other people who may also have a dream yet to be. Through all the tears and laughter, she shares her journey and faith in God living that childhood dream.